RISING STRONG

MOTIVATIONAL TALES OF WOMEN FINDING THEIR INNER STRENGTH

DR. JAGADEESH PILLAI

Made with ❤ on the Notion Press Platform
www.notionpress.com

|| Dedicated to Younger Generation to Motivate ||

Contents

Contents

Prayer

"Om Sahanaa Vavatu Sahanau BhunaktuSaha Veeryam KaravaavahaiTejasvi Naavadheetamastu Maa VidvishaavahaiOm Shantih Shantih Shantih"

The literal interpretation of this mantra is: OM. Let us all protect one another, let us all share in joy, let us all work together and let our learning be illuminated. Let us be united in peace,
OM Peace, Peace, Peace.

❧❧❧

About The Author Of This Book

Dr. Jagadeesh Pillai is a renowned Guinness World Record holder, writer, and researcher hailing from Varanasi, also known as the abode of Lord Shiva. With a Ph.D. in Vedic Science and a range of creative ideas and achievements, he is a true polymath. Although his roots can be traced back to Kerala, the people of Varanasi hold him in high regard and affectionately consider him one of their own.

Dr. Pillai has achieved four Guinness World Records in the following subjects:

1. "Script to Screen" - In this record, Dr. Pillai produced and directed an animation film within the shortest time possible, breaking the previous record set by Canadians. He has also received numerous national and international awards and recognitions for this achievement.

2. Longest Line of Postcards - For this record, Dr. Pillai created a line of 16,300 postcards on the occasion of the 163rd anniversary of Indian Postal Day. The event also included a questionnaire about the Indian flag.

3. Largest Poster Awareness Campaign - Dr. Pillai designed an awareness campaign on the subject of "Beti Bachao - Beti Padhao" (Save the Girl Child - Educate the Girl Child) to achieve this record.

4. Largest Envelope - In tribute to the Indian Prime Minister's "Make in India" initiative, Dr. Pillai created a 4000 square meter envelope using waste paper to achieve this record.

5. Attempted - 70000 Candles on a 210 kg Cake - To celebrate the 70th Indian Independence Day, Dr. Pillai attempted to light 70,000 candles on a 210 kg cake, which was recorded in World Records India.

6. Attempted - Documentary on Dhamek Stupa of Sarnath in 17 Languages - Dr. Pillai attempted to create a documentary on the Dhamek Stupa of Sarnath, dubbing it in 17 different languages. The result of this attempt is currently awaiting confirmation from the Guinness World Records.

He is versatile in Gita teaching. The young generation is fond of his Gita teaching and he has changed the life of many young through his continued motivational boost up and teachings.

He has composed and sung Gayatri Mantra in 1008 different tunes.

He has composed and sung Hanuman Chalisa in 108 different tunes.

He has composed and sung hundreds of Sanskrit Bhajans,

Patriotic songs, etc.

He has written and directed so many short films and documentaries for awareness campaigns.

He has done voluntary services to UP Police and Kerala Police to spread awareness campaigns on the various issue through videos and photography.

He is on the path of authoring thousands of books on Indian culture, Indian Temples, and the life of extraordinary people.

It is hard to believe that he has produced and directed more than 100 Documentaries on a particular city (Varanasi) which is done by a single person.

He has helped and guided more than 25 boys and girls to achieve world records through various creative and innovative methods.

A multifaceted person who can apply the best of his intellect using the God-given blessings which have been showered upon every human being granting them an immense capacity to learn, experience, and experiment with many things and do wonders in this world of discrimination and disparities.

He is a teacher and a student at the same time who always learns every day and teaches every day. As a master, his weakness was that he never sticks to a particular subject. Perhaps this weakness gives him the strength to master any area which he came across.

Each of his days dawned with learning a new topic and he spend most of his time experimenting and researching it.

He is also a selfless social activist and a motivational speaker.

His life was full of struggle, ups and downs, and failures. But he never gave up and faced all his trials and tribulations full of confidence. Today he is a successful young man with a lot of enthusiasm and rich life experience.

He is an efficient Tarot Card Reader, Astro-Vastu Consultant and an excellent singer and composer.

He has sung full Ram Charita Manas 138 hours audio by his own composition. He has also sung the whole Bhagavad-Gita in his own composition with a rhythmic background.

He has also sung "Lokah Samastha Sukhino Bhavantu" in 50 different languages.

Currently working on a detailed and scientific study on Veda, Upanishad, Puranas, Bhagavad Gita, etc.

He has composed and sung Hanuman Chalisa in 108 different compositions and Gayatri Mantra in 1008 different compositions.

Awards - Four Times Guinness World Records, Winner of Mahatma Gandhi Vishwa Shanti Puraskar , Mahatma Gandhi Global Peace Ambassador, Kashi Ratna Award, Dr. APJ Abdul Kalam Motivational Person of the Year 2017,

Mother Teresa Award, Indira Gandhi Priyadarshini Award, Bharat Vikas Ratna Award, Udyog Ratna Award, Vigyan Prasar Award, Poorvanchal Ratn Samman.

Preface

In this book, we present a collection of motivational stories about women who have overcome challenges, pursued their passions, and achieved their goals. These stories come from a variety of sources, including real-life accounts of ordinary women who have done extraordinary things, as well as fictional accounts of women who have faced and conquered adversity.

Each of these stories is unique, but they all share a common theme: the power of the human spirit and the strength and determination of women. As you read these stories, we hope you will be inspired by the resilience, perseverance, and courage of the women featured in these pages.

These stories are meant to serve as a source of inspiration and motivation for all women, no matter what their circumstances or goals may be. We hope that these stories will encourage you to believe in yourself, to pursue your dreams, and to overcome any obstacles that may come your way.

So join us on this journey of discovery as we explore the motivational stories of these remarkable women. May their stories inspire and motivate you to be the best version of yourself, and to achieve all that you are capable of.

1

Evaluation of Skills

Once upon a time there lived a young woman who had big dreams but very few resources. She lived in a small rural village where the opportunities were limited and the future looked bleak with no means of furthering her education and no real way to escape the limited existence of her current fortune. However, she was inspired to keep dreaming and undeterred by the lack of resources, she believed that if she kept searching, she could find a way to make her dreams a reality.

Before she moved on, she took the time to evaluate her goals, assess her current skills, and define her long-term vision. She set a plan in motion to push herself a little further each day, both mentally and physically. She began to learn and acquire new skills that would help her on her journey to make her dreams a reality.

The woman devoted much of her time to learning, taking on any available application or course that could teach her something new. She also began to spend her time researching businesses, industries, and technological advances that could benefit her once she achieved her goals. Despite her lack of resources, she was determined to get the skills and knowledge she needed to succeed.

Additionally, the woman made sure to stay focused on the steps she must take to get closer to her goals. Even if everyone around her thought she was naïve and foolish to follow her dreams, the woman never gave up. She worked twice as hard to prove her doubters wrong and to make her vision a reality.

The woman used her hard work and dedication to manifest new opportunities for herself. She was soon seen as a leader within her community and her determination was admired by all who truly knew her. Her ability to take risks and push herself further than anyone else was her biggest asset, and it helped her build the life she had dreamed of.

The woman continued to make strides in her career and consistently took on new challenges and opportunities that came her way. She soon became an inspiration to those around her, many of them motivated and inspired to move forward with their own dreams. She was the epitome of achieving and navigating through life despite the odds, and this attitude of resilience and encouragement resonated with people who appreciated her drive and vision.

The woman's journey was a testament to how vision and drive can surpass all odds and create a path to success. Even in the face of tremendous obstacles, the woman found a way to make her vision a reality and inspire generations to come. Her short-term and long-term perseverance became her greatest weapon in overcoming all obstacles and fuel the motivation of others.

The woman's story is a profound reminder of the power of resilience and determination, and a motivating inspiration for others. She serves as a source of pride and a reminder that one can achieve so much if they have faith in themselves and never give up. Her strength and determination serve as a source of pride and motivation for others.

2
Reading Inspiring Books

Once upon a time, there was a young woman named Jennifer. She was fresh out of college and still trying to figure out what she wanted to do with her life. She had a vague idea about going into the business world, but she wasn't sure if that's what she wanted to do. One day, her cousin suggested that she take a shot at becoming a motivational speaker, and Jennifer thought it sounded like an exciting adventure.

So Jennifer got to work. She started by researching successful motivational speakers, studying their techniques and practicing her own unique delivery. She read numerous books and articles, studied different techniques on how to resonate with an audience, and began crafting an inspiring message of hope and encouragement.

Jennifer began to build her profile slowly, attending small local events and conferences, enlisting the help of her family and friends at first and then expanding her reach to include new audiences. Everywhere she went, she connected with people and made a positive impact in their lives and communities.

Over time, Jennifer's audience grew and her impacts expanded. People came to her events more and more, often traveling hundreds of miles just to listen to her pass on her stories and advice. Word of mouth spread and soon corporations, universities, churches, and other organizations began contracting Jennifer to speak to their employees and constituents.

She continued to put out her message and fight for justice, equity, and compassion. She experienced her fair share of criticism and failure, but from those hardships she started to build a resilience and dedication. She wasn't afraid to speak up for what she believed in and handle disagreements along the way.

Although Jennifer faced many challenges along her journey, her inspiring message resonated with many people and positively impacted their lives. Those same people then carried on her message and championed her cause. This snowballed into an ever-growing movement of positivity, empowerment and hope.

Today, Jennifer continues to spread her powerful message of inspiration and hope to audiences across the globe. She always reminds her listeners that anything is possible and that they're the only ones in control of their lives. She has become an example of strength and courage, motivation and inspiration.

By never giving up, Jennifer became one of the most sought-after motivational speakers in the world. She plays a significant role in promoting progress and global change, and is reminded daily of the excellence and power within herself and others. Her story is a testament to the potential within by those who are willing to go out and realize their dreams.

ppp

3

Following Dreams

Sara had always been a dreamer. She spent her days lost in thought, imagining the life she wanted for herself and the person she wanted to become. But no matter how hard she tried, it seemed like her dreams were always just out of reach.

Sara grew up in a small town where opportunities were scarce and the only way to get ahead was to work hard and hope for the best. She was the youngest of four children and her parents struggled to make ends meet. They always encouraged her to do well in school and to pursue her dreams, but they didn't have the means to help her achieve them.

Despite the challenges she faced, Sara never let go of her dreams. She worked hard in school and earned good grades, but when it came time to apply to college, she couldn't afford to go. She was heartbroken, but she refused to let her dream die.

After graduating high school, Sara got a job at the local

grocery store to save up money for college. She worked long hours and often had to sacrifice her own needs for the sake of her family. But she never complained. She knew that this was her chance to make something of herself, and she wasn't going to let it slip away.

As the years went by, Sara's determination and hard work began to pay off. She saved enough money to enroll in a community college, and she excelled in her studies. She was determined to make the most of this opportunity and to prove to herself that she was capable of achieving her dreams.

As she moved on to a four-year university, Sara encountered even more challenges. She struggled to balance her studies with her job and her family obligations, and there were many times when she wanted to give up. But she refused to let go of her dream. She knew that she was capable of achieving great things, and she was determined to make it happen.

Finally, after years of hard work and determination, Sara graduated from college with a degree in business. She was thrilled and proud of herself for overcoming all the obstacles she had faced and for achieving her dream.

But Sara's journey was far from over. She knew that she still had a long way to go before she could truly call herself a success. She was determined to make a name for herself in the business world and to create a better life for herself and her family.

And so, with hard work and determination, Sara began to

climb the ladder of success. She started her own business and worked tirelessly to build it into a thriving enterprise. She faced countless challenges along the way, but she never let them get in her way. She knew that she had the talent and the drive to succeed, and she was determined to make it happen.

As the years passed, Sara's business continued to grow and thrive. She became a leader in her industry and an inspiration to all who knew her. She had achieved her dream and so much more, and she did it all through hard work, determination, and a refusal to give up.

Today, Sara is a successful businesswoman and a role model for women everywhere. She has proven that with hard work and determination, anything is possible. And she continues to inspire others to chase their dreams and to never give up, no matter how difficult the journey may seem.

ppp

4

Keeping Motivated

Claire was a single mother of two and due to her limited income, she struggled to make ends meet. Despite her financial situation, she was determined to provide a better life for her children and to make something of herself. Whenever she had the chance, she studied hard, trying to gain the knowledge necessary to become successful.

One day, she came across a job posting that offered her the chance to make a decent salary in a small, but well-known company. Excited, she applied, and a week later, was invited for an interview. Despite her nerves, she was determined to land this job and knew she had what it took. She was enthusiastic, upbeat, and confident as she entered the room.

After a few minutes of gruelling questioning, she was offered the position. Claire was thrilled, and couldn't help but feel proud of her accomplishments. She was determined to make this job work, and devoted her time, energy and enthusiasm to her work, no matter the task.

Most of the people she worked with were supportive and encouraging, while there were a few who were less than kind. Claire knew she had to stay strong and ignore the negativity to keep her focus on her goal.

No matter how tired or discouraged she became, reminding herself of why she was doing this – for her children – kept her motivated and determined. She worked hard to make sure her children never felt the sting of poverty, and dreamed of a better future for them.

Eventually, her hard work paid off. After a few years, her financial situation improved, allowing her to provide a more comfortable life for her children. She was able to quit her second job, her children had a higher quality of life, and she even was able to save for their future.

Claire was grateful for all of the opportunities that had been afforded to her and for the hard work she had put in. This hard work was rewarded and due to the people around her, the support of her family and the determined attitude that she maintained, she was able to make her dreams a reality and provide a better future for her family. Her story is one of determination and perseverance, and a reminder that despite the odds, you can make it!

5

Path to Self-Motivation

The sun shone brightly onto an empty street as a woman hurried to reach her destination. Her heart fluttered with excitement as she thought about the possibilities that awaited her. She thought back to how far she had come. From the moment she was born, life had thrown her many challenges. Despite growing up in poverty, she had never allowed herself to be defined by her circumstances.

The woman could remember the many late nights, when she had curled up on the couch with a pen and paper. She would pour all her feelings of despair, frustration and determination onto the page. Through self-reflection and wordplay, she discovered a path to self-motivation.

With this newly discovered tool, she began to reconstruct her life and her future. She had no idea how long it would take or how much hard work it would require but she was sure of one thing: she would never give up.

Every morning, the woman rose early and jotted down her goals for the day. She consistently worked hard to achieve these goals, no matter how small or large. From early successes, she grew in confidence and gathered the courage to overcome bigger challenges.

But she wasn't solely dependent on her own strength. As the woman set out on her path, she met inspiring people who also believed in her and helped her to reach further. Through these relationships, she became part of a strong, positive network.

Slowly but surely, this motivated woman started to build a future of her own design. The more determined she became, the more her abilities began to show. She pushed herself to read more and stay up to date with ever-evolving trends.

With each passing day, she inched closer and closer to her ultimate dream. One day, after much hard work and dedication, she opened her very own business.

The woman was now a successful entrepreneur. She achieved success not by relying on others, but by relying on herself. She drew inspiration from her past and tapped into her forgotten reservoirs of motivation to help her reach greater heights.

Today, the woman stands proud as a living example of what can be achieved through perseverance and determination. As she looks back at the long road she has walked, she remembers the importance of believing in oneself and never giving up.

Her journey has been a reminder that no obstacle is too great and that motivation can come from unexpected places. May her story serve as an inspiration for women everywhere, that no dream is too far-fetched and that we should never settle for mediocrity.

ᔕᔕᔕ

6

Determination

Once there was a woman named Sarah who lived in a small town in the countryside. Sarah had always dreamed of making a difference in the world, but she felt trapped by her circumstances and limited by her own self-doubt.

Despite these challenges, Sarah refused to give up on her dreams. She knew that with hard work and determination, anything was possible.

One day, Sarah decided to take a chance and applied to a prestigious university in the city. To her surprise, she was accepted and offered a full scholarship.

Excited for the opportunity to pursue her passions, Sarah packed her bags and headed off to the city to start her new life.

At the university, Sarah threw herself into her studies, determined to make the most of every opportunity that came her way. She worked hard and excelled in her classes, earning top grades and the respect of her professors.

As she progressed through her studies, Sarah discovered her true passion – environmental science. She became deeply interested in the ways in which humans were impacting the planet and dedicated herself to finding solutions to the world's most pressing environmental problems.

Despite facing many challenges and setbacks along the way, Sarah refused to give up. She spent long hours in the library, conducting research and writing papers. She also participated in a number of extracurricular activities, including a student-led environmental group on campus.

Through her hard work and dedication, Sarah eventually graduated at the top of her class. Her professors were so impressed with her achievements that they recommended her for a coveted internship at a renowned environmental research organization.

Sarah eagerly accepted the opportunity and spent the summer working alongside some of the world's leading experts in the field. She learned so much and made valuable connections that would serve her well in her future career.

Upon completing her internship, Sarah was offered a full-time position at the organization. She was thrilled to be able to continue her work in the field that she was so passionate about.

Over the years, Sarah worked tirelessly to make a difference in the world. She traveled to remote corners of the globe, conducting research and working with local communities to protect the environment.

Through her efforts, Sarah helped to preserve some of the world's most precious natural resources and made a lasting impact on the planet.

Sarah's story is a testament to the power of hard work and determination. She never let her circumstances or self-doubt hold her back, and instead pursued her dreams with fierce determination. And in the end, she achieved greatness and made a meaningful difference in the world.

ϷϷϷ

7

Commitment Towards Goal

❦

Once upon a time, there was a woman who knew she could do anything. She was confident and determined, never hesitating to take risks or try something new.

This woman had been blessed with ambition and drive; nothing was impossible for her to achieve. She had the courage to attempt difficult tasks, applying those abilities to create amazing results.

Despite her natural abilities, the woman often found herself held back by society's expectations and gender roles. In her culture, it was expected that a woman stay at home, keep quiet, and adhere to the standards set by her elders. But she refused to conform.

From an early age, the woman had dreamed of going out into the world and making her own way. She wanted to live an extraordinary life, to explore, to encounter amazing things and have amazing experiences. She wanted to be able to make a difference in the lives of those around her, to both enrich and change them for the better.

The woman knew that her dreams were big, too big for her culture to accept. But she refused to let that reality stop her. She combated her doubts, fears, and insecurities with a deep belief that she could do anything she set her mind to.

When she was just starting out, she found success in the tiniest of actions. By committing to her goals, she managed to make progress even when it seemed impossible. Each success, no matter how small, was a huge motivation for her, propelling her further on her journey.

Eventually, her efforts began to pay off. She found herself working in a job that made her truly happy, making a real difference in the world. With a newfound courage, she used her skills and experience to go even further, chasing down opportunities and creating amazing things.

In time, she found herself in a place where she could focus on designing her own future. She started off with simple projects, commissioning the creation of books that were meaningful to her, planning events that had both social and spiritual significance, and finding unique ways of connecting with her local community.

The woman was now living her best life – a life that was both meaningful and powerful. In everything she did, she put her heart, mind and soul into it, ensuring that everything was of the highest quality. Her hard work and determination were paying off.

The woman was a role model for her peers, inspiring them to follow their dreams and use their own talents to make the world better. She encouraged people to think outside of the box and chase their passions, educating herself and others on what it means to really live an extraordinary life.

This woman stands today as a testament that ambition and courage are unstoppable forces. She dared to be brave, take risks, and live an extraordinary life. If she can do it, then anyone can.

ᗞᗞᗞ

8
Impact of Motivational Quotes

—♡—

Once upon a time there was a woman named Rose, who was a strong and determined individual. She had dreams and ambitions for the future and worked hard to achieve them. But no matter how much she worked, it seemed like she was falling short of success.

So one day, she decided to make a change. She was going to be a more motivated and determined person, so she began to set mini-goals and set the bar higher everyday.

With the help of her family, friends, and mentors she set out to create a plan to change her current situation. She started off small, making little changes in her day to day activities that would lead her down the path of success.

Rose woke up early each morning and made time for yoga, stretching and running to start her day off right. She followed a strict diet and began to eliminate any bad habits or negative thoughts.

Rose implemented a daily schedule and budgeted with precision. She also found the time to volunteer and do some community service here and there to give back.

On days when Rose felt like she was losing motivation and progress was slow, she would look up motivational quotes and speakers to keep her going. She also made sure to take breaks and spend time with her friends and family.

With so much hard work and determination, Rose was beginning to see the results. She was now ahead of schedule and her goals were almost within reach.

Rose kept pushing forward, kept the faith and kept working hard. She surrounded herself with positive energy and like minded people, who kept her disciplined and determined. She also began to use affirmations and reading inspiring stories to boost her morale.

And before long, Rose achieved her goals. She was now a successful woman who set an example for everyone around her. By believing in herself and following her dreams, Rose has become an embodiment of determination and strength.

Rose is an example of what we all can achieve. With hard work and determination, anyone can exceed their own expectations and overcome any challenges and obstacles that might come their way.

ᗞᗞᗞ

9
Reaching New Heights

When Yumi entered the room she immediately knew the stakes were high. She felt the eyes of her peers prying her as she walked up to the front and took her place before the intimidating crowd. She was a woman with a strong heart, and an even stronger drive to succeed. She spoke with conviction as she explained her vision of the future she would create with her groundbreaking research. Many applauded her efforts, but even more were evidently skeptical of her ability to accomplish such a feat of daring. Unfazed, Yumi carried on with the presentation and addressed the crowd with the same confidence she'd had when she entered the room. After what felt like an eternity, her presentation was finally over.

The room lulled in silence as everyone punctuated every syllable she said. A few timid hands were raised as questions were posed to her. Yumi felt her heart racing in her chest, yet her composure never faltered. Replying to each inquiry with poise and clarity, Yumi gave the audience examples of how the past inspired her and how the research she was proposing had already yielded tangible results. The room erupted in applause as the presentation came to a close.

Yumi took a deep breath and let out a smile. She had done it. In a single day she had gone from a scientist with a revolutionary idea to becoming a champion for change. It was a dream she had had for many years and now it was finally coming to fruition. It had taken immense amounts of hard work, discipline, and dedication to make this moment a reality, but Yumi never once forgot her end goal: furthering human understanding and improving the lives of all.

As the audience dispersed, Yumi was met with numerous well wishers who praised her efforts. She beamed with joy as she expressed her gratitude and humbly accepted their compliments. But the moment was brought to a halt when one of her peers caught her attention: "So, when do you plan to start?"

Yumi laughed and replied, "Right now."

This comment marked the start of Yumi's incredible journey. She devoted every hour of her day to her work, and as her research progressed so did her confidence. She held herself to higher standards and pushed her limits in ways she never thought possible. With each breakthrough she achieved, Yumi's conviction grew stronger and she was determined to reach new heights in her field.

The days flew by, and soon Yumi's research became the talk of the town. Everyone was fascinated by the creativity and innovation she brought to the field. Even her skeptics had changed their tune and respected her incredible accomplishments. Her dedication served as an inspiration to many people, and her message of resilience and ambition resonated with women everywhere. Yumi gathered an entire following eager to emulate her success, yet she never once rested on.

ᗡᗡᗡ

10
Determined to Succeed

Lena was a young woman who lived in a small village on the outskirts of a bustling city. She was intelligent and ambitious, but her circumstances seemed to be holding her back.

Growing up, Lena's family was poor and they struggled to make ends meet. Despite this, Lena was determined to succeed and worked hard in school. She excelled in her studies and was often top of her class, but she knew that she wanted more out of life.

One day, Lena came across a flyer for a scholarship program at a prestigious university in the city. She knew that this was her chance to break free from the constraints of her village and pursue her dreams.

Determined to succeed, Lena applied for the scholarship and spent hours pouring over her application, perfecting every detail. When the results were announced, Lena was thrilled to find out that she had been selected as one of the recipients.

Excited for the opportunity to attend university, Lena packed her bags and headed to the city. She was intimidated by the new environment, but she was determined to make the most of her opportunity.

At the university, Lena excelled in her studies and became deeply involved in a number of extracurricular activities. She joined a student group that worked on social justice issues and spent her free time volunteering at a local soup kitchen.

As she progressed through her studies, Lena discovered her passion for activism and social justice. She became deeply committed to creating positive change in the world and worked tirelessly to make a difference.

Despite facing numerous challenges and setbacks along the way, Lena refused to give up. She persevered and eventually graduated at the top of her class.

After graduation, Lena landed a job at a non-profit organization where she worked to advocate for disadvantaged communities. She poured her heart and soul into her work and made a real impact in the world.

Lena's story is a testament to the power of determination and hard work. She never let her circumstances hold her back and instead pursued her dreams with fierce determination. And in the end, she achieved greatness and made a meaningful difference in the world.

ᗧᗧᗧ

11
Inner Sense of Peace

Once upon a time, there lived a woman named Sarah who was deeply passionate about her career and her dreams. She had been working in the same job for a few years and while she was respected in her profession, she wasn't always fulfilled. She dreamt of bigger and better things but was too afraid to try and pursue them. One day, she made the decision to take the plunge and try something new.

Sarah worked hard to do research on her dream job and worked out her action plan to make it happen. She read up on different career paths and read a ton of books on the subject. She also reached out to people in the same field and based on their advice, she started to take small steps towards her goal. First, she signed up for a short course that was relevant to her desired job. She also attended networking events, seminars and conferences related to the field.

Sarah soon started feeling the satisfaction that she was looking for in her career. She felt an inner sense of peace, having undertaken this journey of her own accord and that too fearlessly. But she also knew that this was just the beginning and she had to keep going. She realized that as her journey in her dream career goes on, there will be challenges that she has to face and obstacles to overcome.

To help herself stay motivated and driven towards her goal, Sarah kept track of all the progress she was making and all the milestones she had achieved. She made a list of all her achievements, no matter how small they were, to remind her of her success even in the darkest moments. This practice made her feel more confident in her ability to succeed.

Every day Sarah was growing both professionally and personally. With every day came a new level of love for her dream job and a stronger commitment to realize her dreams. She also started to recognize her own potential and inner strength that was leading her onward.

As Sarah's journey went on more and more people began to recognize and appreciate her efforts, helping her to stay motivated on her pursuit. Through her hard work and dedication, she eventually became a part of the team she had always wanted to be a part of and her dream career was becoming a reality.

Sarah's story highlights the importance of hard work, dedication and commitment. She reminds us that if you believe in yourself and have the courage to try, you can achieve anything. If she could have the courage to take the plunge to pursue her dreams, there's nothing we can't achieve. Sarah is a source of motivation and a reminder that no matter what challenges come our way, with determination and belief, we can reach our goals.

❥❥❥

12
Staying True to Her Dreams

Once upon a time, there was a young woman whose ambition and drive knew no bound. From a young age, she was determined to leave a mark on society and make a difference to the lives of those around her.

At eighteen, she decided to take on a challenge that started with a simple yet audacious goal: to own her own business by the time she was twenty-five. This was a daunting task at the time, as the world outside was harsh and the journey to success was long, with no guarantee of glory at the end.

But the young woman was determined. She studied day and night and improved her skills over time. She worked hard and stayed focused. She did not stop when she failed and kept trying.

Despite her brilliance and her work ethic, she still encountered several roadblocks. Many frowned upon her ambition, believing that she should focus on marriage and be content with a 'traditional' role.

But she persevered, brushing off the comments and staying true to her dreams. She knew that she had to make sacrifices to be successful, and she was willing to accept them.

After years of effort and hard work, the young woman finally managed to launch her own business. Starting small, she began with just a few products and services. From there, gradually her business expanded, and before long, she was running a successful enterprise.

Every step of the way, she credited all her success to the resilience and hard work she had put into her journey. From all her trials and tribulations, she learnt that to achieve her dreams, she must never give up.

Today, that young woman is a role model for those who wish to find success. She often visits schools and business establishments, delivering speeches and speeches, offering words of wisdom and motivation.

Her messages are clear and simple: have faith in yourself, stay determined and never let anyone tell you what you can or cannot do. Whatever you set your mind to, it can be achieved.

The young woman is a beacon of hope, a source of motivation, a symbol of resilience and tenacity. She reminds us that nothing is impossible and that success is within our grasp if we just keep our eyes on the prize.

ᐺᐺᐺ

13
Discovering True Passion

Emma was a young woman who lived in a small town on the coast. She had always been passionate about the ocean and spent her days surfing and exploring the coastline.

Despite her love for the ocean, Emma knew that she wanted more out of life. She was intelligent and ambitious, and she dreamed of making a difference in the world.

One day, Emma came across an opportunity to study marine biology at a prestigious university on the other side of the country. She knew that this was her chance to pursue her dreams and make a difference.

Excited for the opportunity, Emma applied for the program and spent hours perfecting her application. When the results were announced, she was thrilled to find out that she had been accepted.

Emma packed her bags and headed off to the university, determined to make the most of her opportunity. She excelled in her studies and became deeply involved in a number of extracurricular activities, including a student group that focused on ocean conservation.

As she progressed through her studies, Emma discovered her true passion – protecting the ocean and its wildlife. She became deeply committed to finding solutions to the world's most pressing environmental problems and worked tirelessly to make a difference.

Despite facing numerous challenges and setbacks along the way, Emma refused to give up. She persevered and eventually graduated at the top of her class.

After graduation, Emma landed a job at a leading ocean conservation organization. She poured her heart and soul into her work, traveling to remote corners of the globe to conduct research and protect the ocean.

Through her efforts, Emma helped to preserve some of the world's most precious marine ecosystems and made a lasting impact on the planet.

Emma's story is a testament to the power of passion and hard work. She never let her circumstances hold her back and instead pursued her dreams with fierce determination. And in the end, she achieved greatness and made a meaningful difference in the world.

ppp

14

Focus on the Positive Aspects

Once upon a time, there was a young woman who was going through a difficult stage in her life. She had no direction, and no idea what she wanted to do or where she wanted to go. She was drifting through life, feeling lost and disconnected from the world around her. It seemed like there was no hope, and no way out.

But one day, something changed. The young woman stumbled across a poster that was advertising a motivational course. It promised to help her find her own motivation and create a new perspective on life. She remembered how excited she had been when she first learned about the course and decided to take a chance on it.

When the woman attended the course, her life changed completely. With the help of her new instructors, she began to figure out who she wanted to be and how she wanted to live. She decided that it was time to take control of her life, and become the master of her own destiny.

The woman quickly realized that the key to success was in setting goals. She made a list of her dreams, and worked hard to achieve them. She worked hard to focus on the positive aspects of life and make conscious decisions that would help her go forward.

Soon, the woman began to reap the rewards of her hard work. She progressed quickly in her career and started achieving results that she had never dreamed of before. She also began to develop strong relationships with her friends and co-workers. She soon realized that she was capable of more than she had ever thought possible.

Along the way, the woman also began to find more value in herself. She was no longer a young woman searching for direction, she had become someone who was driven and determined to make something of her life.

The woman was living her life by her own terms, and she was absolutely thrilled with the person she had become. Her newfound confidence and motivation spread to everyone around her, and it was clear that she was an inspiration to those who had seen her struggles.

With newfound courage and newfound dreams, the woman had become the master of her own destiny. Nothing could stop her now!

ᗧᗧᗧ

15
No Matter the Challenge, Never Forget to have Faith

Once upon a time, there was a woman who faced seemingly insurmountable odds. Despite her extraordinary circumstances, she rose courageously and faced each challenge with remarkable strength and fortitude.

Her life wasn't easy. She faced adversity of all kinds; poverty, illness, betrayal, and even discrimination. Yet despite it all, she persevered. She refused to be defined by her circumstances and forced herself to find the courage to overcome any obstacle before her.

She was an independent spirit and a driven woman. Her ambition was soaring, yet her resources were limited. Convinced that if she believed hard enough, she could achieve anything she set her mind to, she was undeterred by the long odds and daunting tasks that lay ahead.

Although she faced many setbacks, she never gave up. She accepted each challenge as an opportunity to learn and grow. She worked hard and strived to make each and every moment count.

When she was faced with a difficult situation, she remembered what her mother once said, "No matter the challenge, never forget to have faith. Believe that you have the power to make a difference." She kept those words close to her heart and drew from them the strength and courage to keep going even when the going got tough.

She took action and never allowed herself to become complacent. She knew that true success was rooted in taking action, so she created an action plan and implemented it one step at a time.

She held herself accountable and refused to listen to the negative influences around her. She learned to trust her own intuition and made sure that every decision she made was rooted firmly in her own values and beliefs.

Along the way, she encountered setbacks, but she never allowed them to consume her. Instead, she used those setbacks as motivations to reach her goals.

She refused to give up and always sought out opportunities to keep pushing forward. No matter what her circumstances, she believed deeply in the power of hard work and focus.

This remarkable woman used the pain of her past, as

formidable as it sometimes was, to fill her with determination and strength. She perceived each challenge as a lesson and leveraged her experiences to her advantage. She trusted her instincts and had faith that she could create the life she desired.

And that's just what she did. The woman who once faced seemingly insurmountable odds defied all odds and ultimately found success. Her remarkable story of courage and resilience will serve as a powerful source of strength and motivation for generations to come.

No matter the challenge, never forget to have faith. Believe that you have the power to make a difference.

ᐳᐳᐳ

16
Gaining Experience

As the sun rose over the small town of Millfield, 27-year-old Ava Thompson pulled herself out of bed, feeling more determined than ever. She had always been a go-getter, but today was different. Today was the day that she was going to finally chase her dreams and make them a reality.

Growing up, Ava had always been fascinated by the world of business. She loved the idea of creating something from nothing and watching it grow and thrive. However, she had always felt held back by her circumstances. She was the oldest of three children and her parents had struggled to make ends meet. They had always encouraged her to aim high, but the reality was that they couldn't afford to send her to business school.

Despite this, Ava had never let her circumstances define her. She had worked hard throughout high school and college, taking on part-time jobs and internships to gain experience and save up for her future. And now, with a bachelor's degree in business and a fire in her belly, she was finally ready to make her move.

She showered and dressed quickly, grabbed a cup of coffee, and headed out the door. Her first stop was the local bank, where she applied for a small business loan. She had spent the last year working on a business plan and building a financial model, and she was confident that she had a strong case for funding.

To her delight, the loan was approved, and Ava left the bank feeling like she was on top of the world. She spent the rest of the day putting the finishing touches on her business plan and setting up her office. By the time the sun set, she was ready to go.

Over the next few weeks, Ava worked tirelessly to get her business off the ground. She spent long hours networking and pitching her services to potential clients. She was passionate about what she was doing and it showed.

Slowly but surely, her hard work started to pay off. She landed her first few clients and began to build a strong reputation in the community. As her business grew, so did her confidence. She knew that she had what it took to succeed and she wasn't about to let anything stand in her way.

Over the next few years, Ava's business continued to thrive. She expanded her team and her services, and she became a well-respected leader in the industry. She was proud of what she had accomplished and grateful for the opportunities that had come her way.

But Ava didn't stop there. She knew that there was always

more to learn and more to achieve. She continued to educate herself and stay up-to-date on the latest trends and technologies. She also became actively involved in her community, volunteering her time and resources to support local organizations and causes.

As she approached her 30th birthday, Ava looked back on the journey she had taken and felt a deep sense of accomplishment. She had turned her dreams into reality and she had done it all on her own terms. She was proud of who she had become and excited for all that the future held.

And as she looked ahead, Ava knew that she was just getting started. She was a woman on a mission and she wasn't about to let anything stand in her way.

ԲԲԲ

17

Opportunity

Once upon a time there lived a hardworking, ambitious and compassionate woman named Abigail. She had grown up knowing that she wanted to create a better life for herself, but due to her difficult circumstances, this seemed an impossible dream. Her parents were struggling financially, and she was raised in an environment of poverty and deprivation. Despite the odds stacked up against her, Abigail never gave up hope.

Rather than staying stagnant and accepting her fate, she was determined to make something of herself. She was hopeful and driven, which she used as fuel for her ambitions. She was tireless in her efforts to achieve her goals, but was often met with closed doors and a lack of opportunity. In spite of this, Abigail continued to persist, believing that with effort and determination, anything was possible.

One day, Abigail heard about a local business opportunity from her cousin. She wasn't sure it was the right choice for her, but she decided to take a chance. She applied for the job and, although it was a struggle, eventually secured the role. Abigail worked diligently and began to build a reputation as a reliable and capable employee.

Over time, her hard work paid off. Her employer was impressed by her dedication and commitment to her work, and soon began to offer her more responsibility. Abigail readily accepted and was eager to seize the opportunity. As she continued to grow, she learned more and more about the business, as well as the industry in general.

In no time, Abigail had become a valued and indispensable member of her team. Her peers recognized her dedication and skills and showed her a great deal of respect. With enough hard work, she was even able to secure a promotion to a managerial position.

Her success inspired those around her, including her family and friends. She was able to use her knowledge and newfound position to help others, especially those in her community. Abigail represented a role model for others in similar positions, which was highly motivating for them, too.

Abigail's remarkable journey was a testament to the power of hard work and perseverance. She had turned her impossible dream into something tangible and real, and this was a source of great pride for her. Whenever times got tough, Abigail would remember her journey and use it as motivation to keep her going.

Abigail's story is one of courage, ambition, and resilience. Her story is a reminder of what is possible when you never give up, even in the face of hardship and adversity. Abigail's story is a true example of how you can make the impossible happen and should be seen as an inspiration for all.

ᐅᐅᐅ

18
Reaching for Greatness

Tori was a woman facing a seemingly insurmountable challenge. She had been laid off from her job, her savings had nearly depleted, and she had no idea how to make her dreams become a reality. Though surrounded by adversity and doubt, she refused to let it consume her. Instead, Tori dug deep and found within her an inner strength to propel her forward.

It started with a single thought, a thought that she had carried with her since she was a little girl: "I'm capable of greatness." This thought drove her to take action, however small it may have seemed, to begin her journey. She reached out to her network of family, friends, and colleagues, asking for help and advice. With their support, she took a few small steps towards achieving her goals.

Tori applied to and was accepted at a local college. There, she enrolled in classes that were outside of her comfort zone. She embraced difficult topics, such as computer science and business, with enthusiasm and a quiet confidence. Despite the challenging coursework, Tori found success. She put in extra effort, spent hours studying and practicing her skills, and formed relationships with her professors.

With a 3.9 GPA and newfound confidence, Tori was ready to take the next step towards reaching her goals. She began to network, setting up informational interviews with people in her dream field. Using these contacts, she was able to acquire internships and jobs, first as a trainee and then as a full-time employee. Through hard work and dedication, she quickly moved up the corporate ladder and eventually found herself in a senior leadership position with a well-respected organization.

Throughout her long journey, Tori was reminded of her initial thought, "I'm capable of greatness." Looking back, she saw how far she'd come and how she'd persevered through all the difficulties that had come her way. She was able to create a path for herself, driven by her own ambition, and she'd made her dream a reality.

Tori's story isn't one of overnight success, but rather a remarkable story of resilience and dedication. She found within herself the power to keep going even when the odds were stacked against her, and it was that inner strength that carried her to greatness. Tori is proof that no matter how difficult the journey, it is possible to make our dreams come true as long as we reach for them with unwavering determination.

ppp

19
Determined to Make a Difference

There was once a woman named Mary who had always dreamed of making a difference in the world. She was driven and ambitious, and she worked hard every day to achieve her goals.

Mary was a talented graphic designer, and she had always dreamed of starting her own design firm. She had a unique style and a natural talent for creating beautiful and effective designs.

Despite her many skills and talents, Mary faced many challenges on her journey. She struggled with self-doubt and often felt like she wasn't good enough. She worried about failing and about not being able to achieve her dreams.

Despite these challenges, Mary refused to give up. She knew that she had something special to offer the world, and she was determined to make a difference no matter what.

Mary worked hard every day, pouring her heart and soul into her work. She learned as much as she could about her craft, and she constantly sought out new opportunities to grow and learn.

As time passed, Mary's hard work and determination began to pay off. She started to gain a reputation as a talented designer, and she started to get more and more work.

Eventually, Mary's dreams started to come true. She was able to start her own design firm, and she quickly became one of the most successful designers in the industry.

But Mary didn't stop there. She was constantly looking for new ways to make a difference, and she used her success to help others. She started a mentorship program for young designers, and she donated a portion of her profits to charity.

Mary's story is a true testament to the power of hard work, determination, and the never-ending pursuit of one's dreams. She showed that with perseverance and a positive attitude, anything is possible.

Mary's journey was not always easy, but she never let that hold her back. She knew that she had something special to offer the world, and she was determined to make a difference no matter what.

So if you're feeling down or like you can't achieve your dreams, just remember Mary's story. With hard work and determination, you too can overcome any obstacle and make your dreams a reality.

ଡଡଡ

20

Perform with Excellence

Miguel had always dreamt of a life in which she could be the one in control, of her own success and her future. She was driven, determined and passionate; the type of woman who wasn't afraid to take a risk or embrace a challenge. She had an unyielding pursuit of excellence that pushed her beyond her comfort zones and saw her rise to success.

But her ambition was hard won. Growing up, Miguel faced numerous barriers and faced a challenging home life - something that would leave its mark in the form of low self-esteem, something she had to learn to tackle.

Though she didn't always have the self-belief, Miguel powered through and the journey was rewarding. She found her time with her grandmother transformative, who reminded her of her value. She then filled her life with travel, learning and experiences to better herself, embrace a broader perspective and increase her self-confidence.

Miguel eventually found her passion, working in finance and developing her career in the financial sector from a trainee start to a senior role in her organisation. She worked long hours and refused to compromise on her standards, leading to numerous promotions. She finally felt that the hard work was paying off, and her skills and confidence were growing exponentially. Elsewhere, she had taken up a variety of hobbies that fed her passions, giving her a sense of achievement and satisfaction.

Miguel was learning how to be a leader and how to perform with excellence, and these experiences would prove invaluable later on. She bought a property, built trusting relationships and eventually moved into consulting and spread her wings further.

Things got even better - though it took more than determination to get there. As she continued learning and developing, Miguel realised she had to take more risks and make more substantive decisions. Her self-esteem was on the rise and she wasn't afraid to reach higher either.

Her confidence took her to the limits and she started to experience more successes - she was developing a name for herself, her skills and her reputation. It seemed nothing was beyond her capabilities.

Eventually, with enthusiasm, perseverance and dedication, Miguel obtained everything that she had wanted.

Throughout her career journey, Miguel learned to trust her instincts, push her boundaries, overcome her fears and take calculated risks. She was confident and energised from the knowledge that she was in control of her own destiny.

There were undoubtedly moments of self-doubt, fear and insecurity, but when she overcame these, Miguel emerged even stronger. She understood that no one could stop her from achieving her goals and she didn't let anything or anyone stand in the way of her destiny. She was now a woman full of self-belief and motivation and determined to use her skill and drive to benefit her career, her relationships and her life.

Miguel's story was an inspiring tale of tenacity, risk-taking and commitment.

ᐅᐅᐅ

21
make a plan

Once upon a time, there was a young woman named Henny. She had always been an ambitious, hardworking individual since childhood, but she had hit a wall in her career and her ambition was slowly being diminished by a lack of motivation. She felt that she was stuck in the same place and just going through the motions of the everyday grind, but knew deep down that there was more that she wanted to accomplish.

One day, she decided that it was time to make a change. She knew that if she was going to reach her goals, she would have to be fiercely persistent and resilient when it came to keeping focused and motivated. So, Henny decided to make a plan.

First, she decided that if she wanted to stay motivated and energized, she needed to surround herself with positive people. She made it a point to spend time with friends who believed in her and reminded her of why she was working so hard in the first place. These people provided love, support, and a fresh perspective, which kept her motivated when it felt like her progress was moving too slowly.

Henny also started to focus on self-care. She knew that she needed to be in the best mental and physical health in order to reach her goals. She started to prioritize peaceful sleep, and tried to give herself at least 8 hours of restful sleep each night. She also made sure to take regular breaks throughout the day, as well as to practice mindfulness. This not only gave her the energy she needed to stay motivated, but it also taught her to be mindful of her thoughts and feelings, allowing her to be more strategic in her approach to reaching her goals.

Finally, Henny set benchmarks and regularly kept track of her progress. She celebrate even the smallest of achievements, but never became content and decided to always move one step further. Every once in a while, she would treat herself for reaching her goals with small rewards. This motivated her to set new goals and continually challenge herself in order to keep reaching for more.

With a newfound internal drive and the tools she used to stay motivated, Henny was able to reach her goals, one step at a time. Her story is a reminder that with dedication and discipline, hard work and persistence, anything is possible!

Other Books Of The Author

1. The Moments When I Met God
2. Kashiyile Theertha Pathangal
3. GURU GYAN VANI
4. Abhiprerak Gita
5. ASSI SE JAIN GHAT TAK
6. Hopelessness of Arjuna
7. The Soul and It's True Nature
8. Sense of Action (Karma)
9. Action through Wisdom
10. Action through Wisdom
11. THEORY AND PRACTICAL OF EVERY ACTION
12. LOGICAL UNDERSTANDING OF THE SUPREME
13. THE IMPERISHABLE SUPREME
14. Yatra Nishadraj se Hanuman Ghat Tak
15. Yatra Karnatak Ghat se Raja Ghat Tak
16. Yatra Pandey Ghat se Prayagraj Ghat Tak
17. Yatra Ranjendra Prasad Ghat se Dattatreya Ghat Tak
18. YaatraSindhiya Ghat se Gwaliar Ghat Tak
19. Yatra Mangala Gauri Ghat se Hanuman Gadhi Ghat Tak
20. Yatra Gaay Ghat Se Nishad Ghat Tak
21. MAA GANGA, GHATEN EVM UTSAV
22. Ganga Arti Dev Deepavali evam Any Utsav
23. Potentials of Digitalized India
24. VEDIC CONSCIOUSNESS
25. A Brief Introduction to Vedic Science
26. Kashi ke Barah Jyotirling
27. IMPACT OF MOTIVATION
28. Let's have a Milky Way Journey
29. Color Therapy in a Nutshell

30. Rigveda in a Nutshell
31. Yajurveda in a Nutshell
32. Samveda in a Nutshell
33. Atharva Veda in a Nutshell
34. Ayushman Bhava - Ayurveda
35. Srimad Bhagavad Gita and Upanishad Connection
36. Srimad Bhagavad Gita - an attempt to summarize each chapter.
37. Facts and Impact of Nakshatra
38. Astro Gems - NAVARATNA
39. Ekadashi - A Concise Overview
40. A Concise View of Hanuman Chalisa
41. Inspirational Gita
42. Nakshatraranyam
43. Summary of 18 Mahapuranas
44. Synopsis of 18 Upa Puranas
45. Rigvediya Upanishads
46. Shukla Yajurvediya Upanishads
47. Krishna Yajurvediya Upanishads
48. Samavediya Upanishads
49. Atharvavediya Upanishads
50. The Seven Great Sages
51. From Rocket Scientist to President Dr. APJ Abdul Kalam
52. The Visionary's Voice - Quotes of Dr. APJ Abdul Kalam
53. The Wisdom of Swami Vivekananda: Insights and Inspiration from a Legendary Spiritual Teacher
54. Ayurvedic Remedies from the Garden
55. Sages and Seers

ॐॐॐ

Contact

DR. JAGADEESH PILLAI

PhD in Vedic Science

Four Times Guinness World Record Holder

Winner of Mahatma Gandhi Vishwa Shanti Puraskar and
Global Peace Ambassador

Gemology, Astro & Vastu Consultant - Spiritual Counselor

Consultant for designing World Record Ideas

Efficient Tarot Card Reader

9839093003

myrichindia@gmail.com

drjagadeeshpillai@facebook

drjagadeeshpillai@instagram

jagadeeshpillai@youtube

www. JAGADEESHPILLAI.com

|| LOKAHA SAMASTHAHA SUKHINO BHAVANTU ||